Glendale Library, Arts & Culture Dept.

890100557 94883

CHILDREN'S ROOM

D0099672

NO LONGER PROPERTY OF
GLENDALE LIBRARY,
ARTS & CULTURE DEPT.

Our Father

Our Father

Written by Rainer Oberthür
Illustrated by Barbara Nascimbeni

Translated by Bob Gaudet
Edited and abridged by Rachel Bomberger

EERDMANS BOOKS FOR YOUNG READERS

GRAND RAPIDS, MICHIGAN / CAMBRIDGE, U.K.

j 242.722 OBE

You are human.
You have so many questions:
Where did the world come from?
Why does it exist?
Why am I here?
Why do people die?
What happens afterward?
Each of these questions
starts you asking about God.

You ask: *Where is God?*
You can't see God,
but you can seek God —
in life and in the world,
in the sun, the moon, the stars,
in growing plants and
in every wondrous creature,
in every person that you meet.
Everything can show you
something about God.

You ask: *Why can't I see God?*
God is too big for us to understand —
bigger and more mysterious
than anything we can imagine.
But we can see God through Jesus.
In Jesus, God became human and lived with us.
Jesus is the best picture we have of God.
What a wonderful gift!

You ask: *How can I talk to God?*
You can tell God anything and everything.
Happy things. Sad things.
There are no wrong words. No stupid questions.
God knows what you are feeling and thinking
even before you say a word.
God is always with you.

You ask: *What can I say to God*
when I can't find the words?
You can pray a prayer that Jesus gave us.
It comes from the Bible, and we call it
the Lord's Prayer.
It's a short prayer, but it carries the feelings and thoughts
of the whole world up to heaven.
Jesus prayed it on a mountain, and God was near.
We can pray it alone or with others,
and when we pray, God is near.

Our Father, who art in heaven,
hallowed be thy name.
Thy kingdom come.
Thy will be done,
on earth as it is in heaven.
Give us this day our daily bread,
and forgive us our trespasses
as we forgive those who trespass against us.

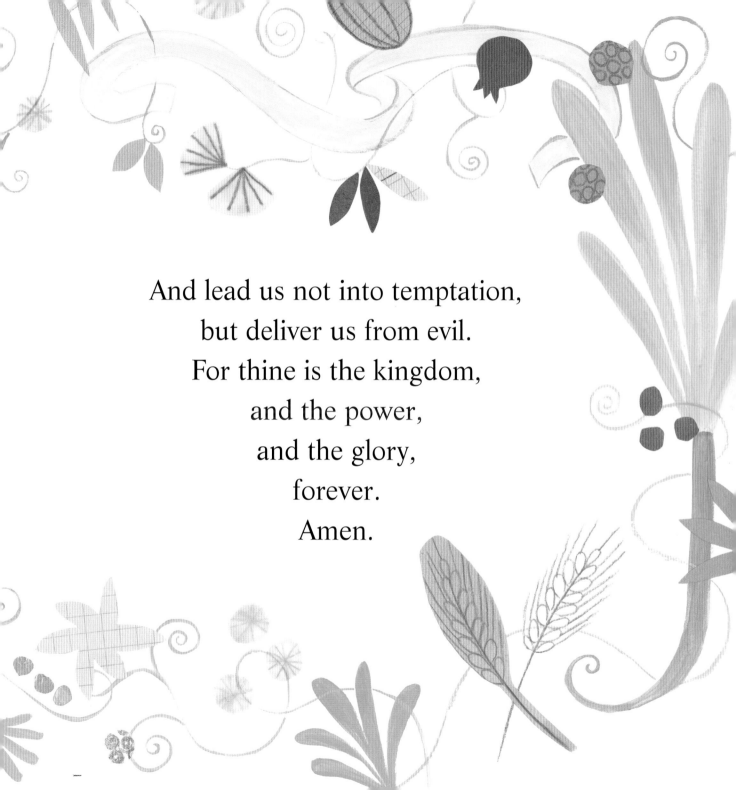

And lead us not into temptation,
but deliver us from evil.
For thine is the kingdom,
and the power,
and the glory,
forever.
Amen.

Father

You are here for us.
You always have been. You always will be.
You created us.
You breathed into us the breath of life —
the same breath that even now fills our lungs.
You are our wisdom. Our light.
Our power. Our peace. Our beauty. Our love.

Our Father

You are *you* to us.

Even though you are bigger than we could possibly begin
to understand, we can call you our Father.

Jesus shows us who you are —

by what he said and did, and by who he is —

and through Jesus, you became part of our human family.

You are like our fathers and our mothers to us.

And yet you are more full of goodness and love

than all the mothers and fathers on earth put together.

Our Father, who art in heaven

We stand and look up at the sky,
and we wonder where heaven is.
But heaven isn't in the clouds, or up in outer space.
It's not a place or a time: it's everywhere.
It's here — where people care for and help each other,
where they see and feel the beauty of creation,
where they live in a way that is right and fair and loving.
Wherever you are, God,
heaven is there.

Hallowed be thy name

You have so many names, God:
You are King and Rock, Savior and Way.
You are Shepherd, Doctor, Friend.
You are our Beginning, our Breath, our Bread.
You are the great Answer to all our questions,
the great Goal of all our hopes and dreams.
You told us you are Yahweh — "I am who I am" —
but still we do not understand.
Even so, we praise your name and call upon it,
just as you call each of us by name.

Thy kingdom come

Your kingdom starts smaller than a tiny seed
and keeps growing with no limit.
We cannot see it, but we can be part of it.
We can find it anywhere and everywhere —
wherever the sick are healed
and the weak are made strong,
wherever tears are wiped away and people laugh for joy,
wherever goodness and love triumph over hate.
Your kingdom has started already,
and someday it will be fully here.

Thy will be done

God, you know us and call us by name.
We have a special place in your heart and in your plans.
Whether we are big or little, poor or rich,
we can each do something for you that nobody else does.
We know that doing what you want
will make us happy —
and make the world a better place, too.
So in our quiet time with you, we ask: What is your will?
Help us to understand your plans and
to walk on the paths that you have marked out for us.

On earth as it is in heaven

You are in the high places and the deep places,
but neither one can hold you.
You are in the very center of the world
and out beyond its farthest edges.
Near and far, high and low —
all things come from you.
Birds always find air, wherever they fly.
Fish always find water, wherever they swim.
And so we find you, our God, everywhere —
wherever our feet walk or our thoughts soar.

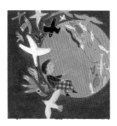

Give us this day our daily bread

We ask you, God, for our bread every day —
we need it to live.
And we ask, too, that you would help us share
with all people what we receive from you.
But we need more than bread for our stomachs.
We need bread for our souls —
a laugh, a hug, a kind word,
a warm sunbeam, a shady tree.
You, Jesus, are the bread that gives us life.

And forgive us our trespasses

In this life, we see both light and shadow,
truth and lies,
good and evil.
We see both right and wrong,
even in our own lives.
We want what is good, but we don't always do it.
Give us courage to look for your goodness
and let it grow in us.
We can be sure that you will never turn your back on us,
no matter what.

As we forgive those who trespass against us

You forgive us,
and so we also want to forgive other people.
Even if we know we are right, we won't reject them.
We won't bring up old hurts,
and we will learn to trust even those
who have harmed us in the past.
We will share your hope and your love.
In this small way, we can show others what you are like:
you are the God of new beginnings.

And lead us not into temptation

We are part of this world —
but we do not belong to it completely.
We belong to God, though sometimes we forget.
Sometimes we let ourselves feel as small as worms
and don't do what we can to help the world.
Sometimes we let ourselves feel as big as God
and try to do more than we should.
Help us, God, to know what we can and cannot do.

But deliver us from evil

You, our God, are stronger than all the evil in the world.
But your strength works differently than we expect.
You came to earth as a tiny baby.
You made yourself small and weak.
You died on a cross for us.
Your strong love —
love that does not need violence to be powerful —
shows us what goodness is.
Your strong love saves us from every evil.

For thine is the kingdom

The whole wide world is yours —
from its beginning to its end and beyond.
Here and now, you are with us.
And someday, there and then, we will be with you.
We dream of the new heaven and the new earth
that you have promised to share with us.

And the power

All that is, is from you.
All that lives and grows and moves comes from you.
On our own, we are so small,
like tiny drops of water in the vast ocean of creation.
But in your love, we are big.
You are our life. Your Holy Spirit lives in us.

And the glory

Everything about you is glorious, strong, and perfect.
You give all things their reason to be.
You are more splendid than the rainbow,
more radiant than the sun.

Forever

You are in your heaven and in our hearts.
You bend down to hear our prayers.
We belong to you, and you care for us.
So it has always been.
So it will always be,
now and forever.

Amen.

Now you know the prayer
that Jesus gave us two thousand years ago,
and you understand at least
a little of what it means.

Millions of people around the world
pray this prayer with you —
young and old,
poor and rich,
happy and sad.
In Jesus' words they find help and comfort.
They turn their hearts to God and live in hope.

You don't need to use lots of big words to talk to God.
It's more important to trust in his love for you
than to worry about using just the right words.
When you look for God, you will always find him.
And as you seek him,
you will start to understand better who you are, too.
Life will become clearer for you,
and you will find peace and courage for every day.

You can read, say, and hear
the prayer of Jesus in another way,
with shorter, simpler words.
Praying this prayer in your own words
can bring you even closer to God.

You, our Father, are near and far.
All that you are — let it be.
All that you want — let it happen,

both in heaven and on earth.
So that we can live,
give us the things we need every day.
So that we can be good,
forgive us when we do wrong
and help us to forgive others.
So that we can learn to want what is right,
do not lead us into temptation.
Instead, save us from every evil.
Amen.

First published in the United States in 2016 by
Eerdmans Books for Young Readers,
an imprint of Wm. B. Eerdmans Publishing Co.
2140 Oak Industrial Dr. NE
Grand Rapids, Michigan 49505
P.O. Box 163, Cambridge CB3 9PU U.K.

www.eerdmans.com/youngreaders

Originally published in Germany in 2013 under the title
Das Vaterunser
by Thienemann Verlag GmbH, Stuttgart/Vienna Germany

Text © 2013 Rainer Oberthür
Illustrations © 2013 Barbara Nascimbeni
© 2013 Gabriel Verlag (Thienemann Verlag GmbH)
English language translation © 2016 Eerdmans Books for Young Readers

Translated by Bob Gaudet
Edited and abridged by Rachel Bomberger

All rights reserved

Manufactured at Tien Wah Press in Malaysia

22 21 20 19 18 17 16   9 8 7 6 5 4 3 2 1

Library of Congress Cataloging-in-Publication Data

Oberthür, Rainer, 1961– author.
[Vater unser. English]
Our father / written by Rainer Oberthür; illustrated by Barbara Nascimbeni.
pages cm
Translated by Bob Gaudet.
Audience: Ages 4-8.
Summary: "Our Father explores the meaning behind each line of the Lord's
Prayer." — Provided by publisher.
ISBN 978-0-8028-5468-1
1. Lord's prayer — Commentaries — Juvenile literature.
2. Prayers — Juvenile literature. 3. Devotional literature — Juvenile literature.
I. Nascimbeni, Barbara, illustrator. II. Title.
BV232.O2413 2016
242.722 — dc23
2015024242

The illustrations were created with acrylic paint on paper and paper collage.
The display type was set in Prose Antiqua.
The text type was set in Life BT.